KV-144-461

Contents

• To order this book call IDAC 0033 2 31 53 17 60 E-mail: idac.aoc@wanadoo.fr or visit www.calvadosbook.com • Want to know more about calvados? Look out for the larger book: Calvados – the world's premier apple brandy (ISBN 91-631-5546-X)
• Copyright 2005 by Henrik Mattsson and Olle Mattsson • All rights reserved under international copyright conventions • **ISBN 91-631-5545-1**
• Published and produced independently by: www.flavourrider.com • Any inquiries regarding this book: contact@calvadosbook.com • The publisher or the author does not accept responsibility for any consequences arising from the use of this book or information contained therein.

The spirit of Normandy

Horses, cheese and apples...

Normandy is situated north-west of Paris, France. Calvados is an area in the middle of Normandy that also gives its name to the apple brandy from specified areas all over Normandy.

The land of Normandy is not like the rest of France - there are no vineyards! Instead, you find orchards full of small, juicy, tart apples.

The landscape, the people and the weather make Normandy a fascinating land of contrasts.

In the heart of Pays d'Auge, Normandy can be enjoyed from convenient viewpoints over lush valleys. Yet most parts of Normandy are pasture and farmland, like the 'Bocage' with its hedgerows and gentle hills. Normandy's coastline

extends over hundreds of kilometres with steep chalk cliffs, the most famous being the cliffs of Etretat and the D-Day landing beaches. Along the coast towards the peninsulas of Manche and Cotentin, the sea has carved out small coves among the granite cliffs.

The larder at the gates of Paris

In the countryside, Normandy is a farmer's paradise. It boasts fertile

No vines – just orchards. The dramatic Norman coastline and the gentle green hills build up in Pays d'Auge.

soil, predictable rainfall and a humid climate. The harvest and produce from Normandy's pastureland, gardens and orchards are some of the best in France, and indeed the world. Apples, cider and calvados have been a natural part of the Norman way of life for centuries and still are.

For many Normans the tourism industry has become an important income and they welcome visitors to their cellar door sales for produce such as cider, pommeau and calvados. Many a barn or farmhouse has been transformed into a 'gite' (a form of bed and breakfast).

The Château de Saint-Germain de Livet dating from the fifteenth and sixteenth centuries, is one of Normandy's great manor houses. There are guided tours of this furnished fairy-tale castle with turrets in pink and white check stonework.

The five 'departments'

The department called Calvados is situated in the middle of Normandy and includes the towns of Cambremer, Lisieux, Livarot and Pont l'Evêque. The green hills and valleys of the Pays d'Auge are situated in its eastern parts and the countryside is full of orchards and farms with traditional half-timbered houses. Here you will find several of the best producers. Several of these make calvados Pays d'Auge (calvados of the highest controlled quality).

Eure is situated east of Calvados with spectacular landscape of river valleys and Norman villages stretching almost to the gates of Paris. Towards the western border to Calvados, some producers make AOC calvados Pays d'Auge others make AOC calvados.

Manche occupies the west coast region and peninsula with Cherbourg facing the English Channel. Producers there make AOC calvados. Its white sandy beaches, magnificent coastal headlands and landmarks like the incredible 'abbey-island' Mont St Michel typify Manche. Towards the border of Orne and Domfront, pear orchards are common and the producers make AOC calvados Domfrontais.

Orne is a rural landscape of green meadows punctuated by elegant chateaux, stud farms and orchards. Most producers around Domfront use large quantities of pears to make the AOC calvados Domfrontais. Some only use apples and make the AOC calvados.

Seine Maritime is situated between the twisting Seine valley and the white chalk cliffs of the Channel coast. East of Rouen lies an area around Neufchatel where producers make AOC calvados.

To many the image of Normandy is the D-Day landing beaches and a lush green countryside with half-timbered farms surrounded by orchards with grazing milk cows and stud farms. Of course there is so much more to explore.

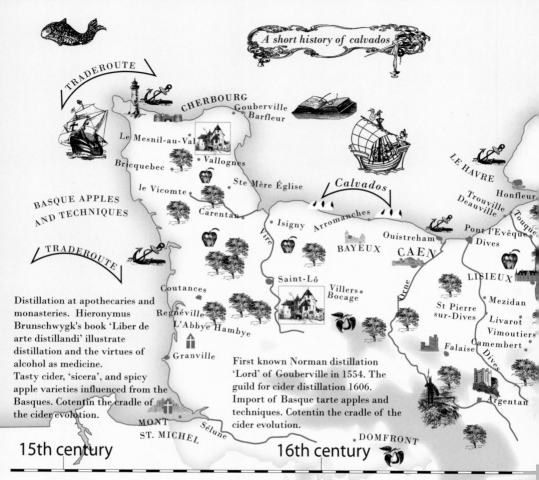

TRADEROUTE

BASQUE APPLES
AND TECHNIQUES

TRADEROUTE

CHERBOURG

Le Mesnil-au-Val

Bricquebec

le Vicomte

Vallognes

Ste Mère Église

Carentan

Goubeville
Barfleur

Isigny

Arromanches

Vire

Calvados

Ouistreham

BAYEUX

CAEN

LE HAVRE

Trouville
Deauville

Honfleur

Touqu

Pont l'Evêque
Dives

LISIEUX

Coutances

Regnéville

L'Abbye Hambye

Granville

Saint-Lô

Villers
Bocage

Orne

St Pierre
sur-Dives

Falaise

Mezidan

Livarot
Vimoutiers

Camembert

Argentan

Distillation at apothecaries and monasteries. Hieronymus Brunschwygk's book 'Liber de arte distillandi' illustrate distillation and the virtues of alcohol as medicine.
Tasty cider, 'sicera', and spicy apple varieties influenced from the Basques. Cotentin the cradle of the cider evolution.

First known Norman distillation 'Lord' of Gouberville in 1554. The guild for cider distillation 1606. Import of Basque tarte apples and techniques. Cotentin the cradle of the cider evolution.

MONT
ST. MICHEL

Sélune

DOMFRONT

15th century

16th century

The area called 'Calvados' was created with the French Revolution. 'Eau de vie de cidre' was called 'calvados' by common man. Mostly a drink for farmers. Output increased.

Output increased with industrial distillation. The working class enjoy 'Café-calva'. Generel interest for natural science. The phylloxera outbreak devastates the vineyards and leads calvados to a 'golden age'.

The cider and apple brandy are of great economic importance in Normandy. Imroved and controlled quality. Centrifugation and filtration.

18th century

19th century

20th century

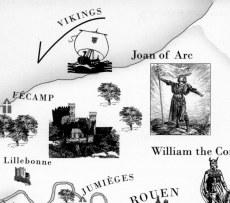

VIKINGS

Joan of Arc

FÉCAMP

Lillebonne

JUMIÈGES

ROUEN

Risle

Audemer

Elbeuf

Le Bec-Hellouin

Thiberville

BERNAY

Broglie

VERNON

EVREUX

SEINE

PARIS

Rugles

William the Conqueror

Celts picked wild apples.

The Romans and monasteries had orchards, and pears were favoured.

0

Martel fought the Muslim Arabs that had knowledge of distillation.

Charlemagne had orchards and brewers.

8th century

Drinking rituals of the Vikings/Normans with ale and 'beor/björr' - fermented apples.

10th century

The press and crushing improves. Inns and merchants sell cider locally called 'succus pomis' or 'pomatium'.

13th century

Battles between English and French. The Black Death and Little Ice Age from the mid-14th through mid-19th centuries. Apples are appreciated. Varieties and orchards are mentioned in several books. Normandy manages thanks to trade and a fertile land. Architectural efforts such as Mont Saint Michel. The rumour of distilled alcohol 'aqua vitae', 'eau de vie' or 'water of life' spread. Raymond Lull and Arnaud de Villeneuve in Montpellier were among the pioneer distillers.

14th century

Expansion of traditional ciderfarms. Cider appears at the tables of the nobles. Taxation and prohibition of cider brandies elsewhere than Brittany, Maine and Normandy.

17th century

Alcohol made for armament. The orchards grow but the quality come to a halt.

The 'Label of origin' in 1942 officially gives calvados its name and protection from the war requisitions.

Reconstruction of cider-houses and distilleries, mainly in the Pays d'Auge. Decline of the traditional farmhouse structures. Modern agriculture with high output.

The remake of the calvados appellation system in 1984. Pommeau gets its recognition in 1991. The cider appellations are refined in 1996. 1997 the appellation for Domfront with 30 % pears take effect.

World War 1   **W.W. 2**   **Post war and modern days**

The 'terroir' of Normandy

A land of contrasts

View over valley in Pays d'Auge (above). Old apple trees (opposite side) in traditional orchard. The temperate and coastal climate combined with the clay soils of Normandy is ideally suited for growing apples, especially in areas like the Pays d'Auge.

The world's premier apple brandy

In theory, all calvados are brandies. Nevertheless, while brandy may be made anywhere in the world, calvados can only be produced in the region in France specified for the appellation of calvados.

'Terroir' of Normandy – a land of orchards

'Terroir' is French for 'soil' but also includes the aspects of geography and weather. It is often used to explain the special taste acquired by a product derived from a certain area. It is the same with calvados.

A particular soil and climate

Western Normandy consists of different layers of sandstone and granites. To the east is the hilly landscape that includes the Pays d'Auge and rests on the limestone plateau of the Paris basin. It has altitudes around 300 metres, split up by erosion forming valleys with clay and flint grounds, perfect for orchards.

The climate in Normandy is west coast marine and is influenced by the North Atlantic and the English

Channel. The summers are fresh with frequent daily weather changes. The warmth of the Gulf stream also results in mild winters. In July, the temperature averages from 14 to 25 °C (57 to 77 °F). Different meso- and microclimates are created in the elevation of the land, valleys and slopes. Forests, rivers, orchards, farmland and hedgerows affect the microclimate. In single orchards, the microclimate can differ at scales of less than hundreds of metres. Factors in the orchard include various tree canopies, aeration, differences in the soil and the angle of the sun.

View over traditional Norman farm with orchards and cows (above). Frequent but short rainfalls are common in Normandy. A rainbow builds up over an orchard (right). The coast towards the Cotentin peninsula (right top). The flat farmland (right) with the hills that mark the start of the Pays d'Auge. The tide (opposite side far right) is strong around the coast and sometimes reach several metres, give rise not only to tasty oysters but also to the phenomena in the Bay of Mont St Michel - where water advances faster than you can walk.

The 'appleations'

Guaranteed tradition and quality

Like most French regional products with unique traditions, calvados is governed by an 'Appellation d'Origine Contrôlée' (AOC) system. It's a set of rules designed to guarantee and maintain the characteristics, production methods and quality of the product and its century-old traditions.

'Haute-tige' high-stem orchard (top left), traditional high-stem orchard with grazing cows (top right), 'basse-tige' low-stem orchard (bottom right, photo from Chateau du Breuil) and 'demi-tige' half-stem orchard (bottom left).

The appellations of calvados

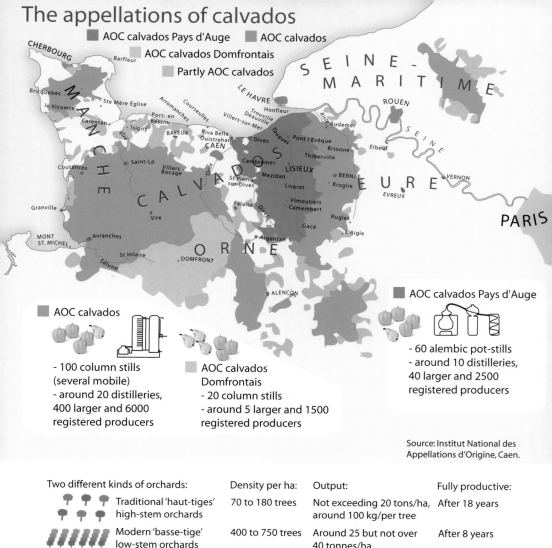

- ■ AOC calvados Pays d'Auge
- ■ AOC calvados
- ■ AOC calvados Domfrontais
- ■ Partly AOC calvados

AOC calvados
- 100 column stills (several mobile)
- around 20 distilleries, 400 larger and 6000 registered producers

AOC calvados Domfrontais
- 20 column stills
- around 5 larger and 1500 registered producers

AOC calvados Pays d'Auge
- 60 alembic pot-stills
- around 10 distilleries, 40 larger and 2500 registered producers

Source: Institut National des Appellations d'Origine, Caen.

Two different kinds of orchards:

	Density per ha:	Output:	Fully productive:
Traditional 'haut-tiges' high-stem orchards	70 to 180 trees	Not exceeding 20 tons/ha, around 100 kg/per tree	After 18 years
Modern 'basse-tige' low-stem orchards	400 to 750 trees	Around 25 but not over 40 tonnes/ha	After 8 years

AOC calvados

The basic appelation

AOC calvados makes up for over 70 percent of the total production.
• Minimum of two years ageing in oak barrels.
• The 'terroir', geographical area, is defined.
• The apples and pears are defined cider varieties.
• The procedures in production like pressing, fermentation, distillation and ageing is regulated.
• Usually single column distillation.

Fermier 'farm-made' calvados

Some quality minded producers both inside and outside the Pays d'Auge make 'calvados fermier', which indicates that the calvados is entirely made on the farm in a traditional agricultural way according to high quality demands.

Calvados Pays d'Auge

Striving for highest quality

When labelled calvados Pays d'Auge the calvados have fulfilled an extensive quality control - the basic rules for AOC calvados together with several additional requirements.
• Ageing for minimum of two years in oak barrels.
• Double distillation in an alembic pot-still.
• Produced within the designated area.
• A minimum of six weeks fermentation of the cider.
• Flavour elements are controlled.

Calvados Domfrontais

Mixing apples and pears

The appellation was created in 1997 and reflects the long tradition of pear orchards in the area, resulting in a unique fruity calvados. The regulation is similar to the AOC calvados and the column still is used.

• A minimum of 30 percent pears from the designated areas is used.

• A three-year minimum of ageing in oak barrels.

• The orchards must consist of at least 15 percent of pear trees (25 percent from the sixteenth harvest).

Pommeau

Sweet blend of calvados and must

Pommeau is a sweet blend made of two-thirds apple juice and one-third calvados. The alcohol level is 16 – 18 percent. Traditionally, to preserve the fruitiest juice all year round, it was mixed with calvados. Since 1991 the pommeau has its own AOC appellation. In general, pommeau is aged for 18 months in oak barrels and have a complex taste reminding of apple, caramel, dried prunes and honey.

The origin of the name

After the French revolution in 1790, the name Calvados was officially given to one of the departments in Normandy. This later gave the name to the apple brandy, first in everyday language in the mid-nineteenth century, and later officially in the appellation in 1942. The question of the origin of the word 'calvados' is not certain. Various assumptions exist and the most widespread is that of a Spanish ship. According to legend a Spanish galleon called 'San El Salvador' or 'San Salvados' was shipwrecked north of the Normandy coast in the middle of the 16th century. The ship's name metamorphosed to calvador and eventually to calvados. However, this story is most likely a myth.

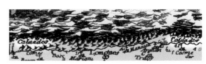

The ship 'San Salvados' at the museum at Père Magloire in Pont-l'Evêque. Part of an old map (below) with the word 'calvados'.

No record of the shipwreck have been found. Instead a word similar to calvados have been discovered on old maps - one from 1675 - indicating two bare rocky points on the high cliffs of Bessin. The word seems to be a mixture of the Latin calvus and dorsum. Together they seem to have marked a place where the rock looked like bald spots from the sea. The sailors located themselves with these 'calvados' and the use of these could have given the area its name.

The label

Blend, year or vintage - three ways to indicate age

The age is mentioned with a certain choice of words and refers to the youngest part of the blend. Some choose to indicate the minimum age in years instead. A blend often contains parts of older calvados. Among higher quality calvados the youngest part of the blend is sometimes much older than mentioned below.

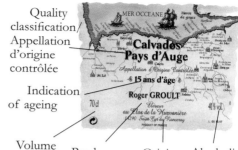

Quality classification / Appellation d'origine contrôlée

Indication of ageing

Volume

Producer or brand name

Origin

Alcoholic strength

Huet (below) use a set of different words to indicate age on their labels while Groult (above) have chosen to indicate the youngest part of the blend in years.

'Fine', 'Trois étoiles ***' 'Trois pommes'	2 years old.
'Vieux' - 'Réserve'	3 years old.
'V.O.' 'VO', 'Vieille Réserve', 'V.S.O.P.' 'VSOP'	4 years old. Often sold older.
'Extra', 'X.O.' 'XO', 'Napoléon', 'Hors d'Age' 'Age Inconnu'	6 years old. Often sold much older.
'1973' (millesime)	The vintage year (the year of distillation).

Vintage

The making

Vapours and selection for aroma and strength

From apple to bottle

The making of truly great calvados is a story of enthusiasm, devotion and the magic of nature. It is a traditional and natural part of the Norman way of farming; practised and refined for generations. Today it is also the story of balancing tradition with modern methods, quality with price and personality with mass production. Many different philosophies and opinions on how a calvados is supposed to be made and what it should taste like exists. Still the final judgment is up to you. Remember it is not just a matter of taste and aroma, but also of atmosphere, occasion and expectation.

The principles for producing calvados are practically the same as other distilled spirits. In the case of calvados, a cider made of apples and pears is distilled. The French stipulate a certain way of making calvados. In short, the apples and pears are picked, ground and pressed to a juice that is fermented into a dry cider, aged and distilled to 'eau de vie'. After two years of ageing in oak casks, it can be sold as calvados. Usually the maturation goes on for several years.

Copper is the most efficient metal to build an alembic. Unlike steel, it is very malleable. It is also a good conductor of heat and reacts in a positive way like a catalyst with the cider. On top of that, it resists corrosion from cider and fire.

Timeline for calvados

The process from apple to calvados take 3 to 4 years, depending on how long the producer ages the cider before distillation.

7. Ageing and blending in oak barrels. Higher quality is aged for many years before bottling (6, 8, 12, 15 and 25 years is not unusual).

3. Fruit maturation. Washing, crushing, pressing the fruit and maceration of the juice.

4. Cider fermentation and ageing of cider. Quality producers age their cider.

5. Distillation from January to June (some distil in autumn as well). Before or after July 1.

1. Growing apples and pears. Orchard maintenance.

WINTER

AUTUMN   SPRING

Start

TIME SUMMER

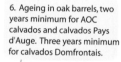

6. Ageing in oak barrels, two years minimum for AOC calvados and calvados Pays d'Auge. Three years minimum for calvados Domfrontais.

2. Harvesting. Mid - October through November and beginning of December.

2 years old AOC calvados, calvados Pays d'Auge

3 years old calvados Domfrontais

0 year old eau de vie

1 year old eau de vie

July 1 - start of countdown

00 year old eau de vie

Picking the
right apple

Worshippers of
sun, rain and air

 **and pear**

It all starts with the apple

The producers only use small apples with great aromatic intensity referred to as cider varieties. Hundreds are typical of Normandy and 48 are recommended in Pays D'Auge. Unlike wine that can be made by a single grape variety, calvados needs the range of tastes and

The apples for cider and calvados are small and tart.

aromas found in different varieties of apple.

The apple varieties are classified into four categories according to their flavour of acidity, sugar content, bitterness and tannin - bitter, bittersweet, sweet or acidulous. Traditional producers grow 20 to 40 varieties while the industrialists use a half dozen mostly acidic and modern varieties.

The varieties of pear are also carefully chosen cider varieties.

By blending different varieties a smooth calvados is created. Usually 10 percent are bitter apple varieties, the majority 70 percent are bittersweet and the rest 20 percent acidic. Acidic apples give the calvados more flavour. In Domfront over 30 percent pears are used and generally results in a fruitier calvados thanks to the sweetness of the pears.

Apple and pear trees are like humans - two 'parent' trees give rise to a new tree and a new variety. To keep varieties, shoots are grafted on selected root stocks. However, they still have to be pollinated to give fruit (photo from Huet).

Making the cider
The cider house rules

Grating, pressing and fermenting

Most of the flavour in calvados is extracted from the skin of the fruit. In the press-house the fruit is crushed or grated. The pulp is left to stand for one to four hours in a vat to macerate (it also changes colour). Around 650 litres of juice is pressed from a ton of fruit. The traditional press is made of wooden trays with linen stacked on each other and pressed together. More effective and hygienic is the adapted version of modern pneumatic presses. The cider is fermented crisp dry in large oak barrels 'tonneau'. The cider ferments for a minimum of six weeks. Quality producers ferment for a longer time and age the cider before distilling it. The minimum alcohol level is 4.5 percent but some producers ferment until 5, 6 or even 7 percent.

Big barrels are used for cider fermentation. After the fermentation, someone has to climb inside and clean it by hand. Today this is done more easily with a pressure washer (photo from Huet).

Fruit per bottle.

18 - 25 kg of fruit.

13 - 15 litres of cider.

One litre of ageing calvados (70%).

Equals around two bottles of calvados 75 cl at 41%.

Based on the fact that one ton of cider apples gives 650 liters of juice.

Apples maturing in a loft (top middle, photo from Drouin), grating the apples (top left, photo from Drouin), washing and rinsing the apples after harvest (top left, photo from Huet), fermenting the must in an oak barrel (right), traditional press (photo from Drouin) and modern pneumatic press (bottom left).

Distilling the cider

Double or single distillation

There are two ways to distil the cider - double distillation in a pot still or continuous distillation in a column still.

The traditional way to fire with wood requires constant attention to regulate

Distillation	Double distillation	Single distillation
• Production	- Complicated - skill, expertise and experience are very important. - Lengthy procedure carried out one batch at a time. - Time consuming.	+ Safe and easy to get right. + Continuous. + Cheap.
• Aroma	+ Complex, delicate and rich fruity aromas.	+ Fruity aroma. - Less complex flavour.
• Ageing	+ Aromas become rounder and develop over the years. + Potential of balance between aromas of apple and oak for longer ageing (10 - 30 years).	+ Take less time to mature. - Gradually vanishing flavour. - Less flavours to evolve with balanced result.

Double distillation of calvados

This is a basic schematic. In addition, different producers all have their own individual secrets to success.

ALAMBIC TRADITIONNEL A CALVADOS

3. A 'chapiteau' (cylindrical bulb) rectifies and stops the cider from boiling over.

1. The 'chauffe-cidre' (pre-heater) contains the next batch of cider, heated by the steam from the still.

COL-DE-CYGNE

VANNE DE VIDANGE

CHAUFFE-CIDRE

EAU DE REFROIDISSEMENT

CHAPITEAU

CHAUDIÈRE

SERPENTIN

VANNE DE VIDANGE

FOYER

EPROUVETTE DE COULÉE

2. The 'la chaudière' (heating-vessel) is heated at 'le foyer' (the hearth) by direct fire using gas or wood.

4. The vapours ascend through the 'col de cygne' (swan's neck) and is cooled through the 'chauffe-cidre'.

5. The final 'réfridgérant' (condenser) is a copper tank with cold water and a serpentine-coil pipe where the alcohol is cooled down and liquefied.

the heat. A chair comes in handy for the night watch at Camut. When firing with wood the surroundings smell of smoke and ageing calvados nearby can pick up some of this aroma. Yet there is not much difference between wood and gas fired spirit at the distilling moment as no smoke enters the closed still. Some producers prefer gas, others wood, and some a combination. Modern alembics use gas that can regulate the heat and thus control the process automatically (see picture of control panel next page).

Sketch on a still at Domaine Dupont used to explain the distillation procedure with heads and tails for visitors. The alembic still at Lecompte (top right) and at Chateau du Breuil (bottom left). The alembic still - a former travelling still - (bottom right) at Domaine 'Coeur de Lion' (Drouin).

Continuous still (next page) for single distillation. Some have wheels to travel the countryside. The cider is preheated in one of the columns, then cooled down and separated in the other. The still can be fed continuously and produces a 'clean' spirit of up to 72 degrees.

The ageing

Time to rest in charred oak

Just after distillation, the calvados has no colour. It is not even called calvados. Instead, it's 'eau de vie de cidre'. Calvados has to gain its name, colour and aromas from ageing. The producers of calvados have agreed to age it for a minimum of two years (three years for Domfrontais). A good deal is aged several years more.

The aroma of fresh apple is wanted in younger calvados but is fundamental for longer maturing calvados. As the calvados gets older, these fruity aromas mature and become balanced with flavours from the oak. One effect of the maturation process is the darkening of the colour caused by oxidation and the high level of alcohol that dissolves colour from the oak.

Time is fundamental but several more conditions influence the calvados like the choice of barrels, the surroundings and the cellar master. The spirit and the barrel interact in unique ways, depending on the type and state of the barrel. For example, a barrel can be new, old or reused. Its inside can be light or heavy toasted. It comes in different sizes and forms. The aeration and aromas in the cellar also have an effect. Finally, the cellar master manages the stock in his

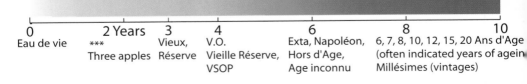

0		2 Years	3	4		6		8		10
Eau de vie		***	Vieux,	V.O.		Exta, Napoléon,		6, 7, 8, 10, 12, 15, 20 Ans d'Age		
		Three apples	Réserve	Vieille Réserve,		Hors d'Age,		(often indicated years of ageing		
				VSOP		Age inconnu		Millésimes (vintages)		

The beautiful cellar at Chateau du Breuil.

individual way.

The young spirit is usually aged in new barrels to give the effect from wood until balanced with the original apple taste. The next step takes place in older barrels where the calvados slowly reaches maturity.

The main desired effects of wood ageing are:
1. Tannins for structure and colour.
2. The reaction with alcohol and wood combined with oxidation that gives aromas reminiscent of dried fruit, caramel, brioche, butter, apricots, banana, coffee, vanilla and cacao.

At Chateau du Breuil (above) and at other producers you can read the level and see the colour of the calvados from vertical measure tubes.

Meet the maitre

Managing the cellar

'Chai' is French for cellar, and 'Maitre' is master. To taste, assemble and blend the calvados is the cellar master's job. The cellar master carefully follows the elaboration in the barrels, constantly checking their maturity, making the necessary decisions and transfers calvados from young to old barrels. To assure the richness, balance and a continuous quality, the calvados is blended. The blend reflects the personal style and taste of the producer or brand. Usually older more complex and coloured calvados is used to give younger, more fruity calvados, the right character, roundness and finesse.

Before bottling, the producer dilutes the level of alcohol to

Small 'fûts' barrels at Boulard and Lecompte speed up the process of maturation.

around 40 – 43 percent alcohol by volume. Some old calvados is sold 'non reduit', not reduced. Occasional 'millesimes' (vintages) are not blended. A vintage calvados should only be bottled if the barrel is outstanding and balanced enough on its own.

Thirsty angels

The evaporation through the wood gives rise to the myth about the share of the angels. Through the pores of the wood, the calvados evaporates. However, it is not all bad, because of this, the aromas get more intense, complex and concentrated. The part that evaporates is called 'part des anges' (the share of the angels). These angels seem to be quite dehydrated and represent an annual loss of about 1 to 3 percent in volume. In small barrels, the loss can rise to 6 percent.

Old barrel at Camut (above) with measure tube. Coopering 'tonnelerie' at Desfrieches in Pays D'Auge (right). Barrels are still handmade though modern tools are used. Different kinds of oak (right) have distinctive qualities

BARRELS OF CALVADOS

Fûts, 220 to 400 litres.

Foudre, from 1000 to 6000 litres.

Cuvé Tronconique, more than 2000 litres.

according to the density of its fibres. Oak is unique in its ability to hold a liquid and at the same time allow it to breath. The level of charring (right, photo from Desfrieches) also affects the calvados. Different kinds of bottles only affect the consumer.

NEVERS · VOSGES · ALLIER ·

TRONÇAIS· LIMOUSIN·

Tasting

Oak resin and apple tart

Calvados, cider and pommeau make perfect match for a lot of food. The French 'À la tienne' (cheers) refers to both family and health. The traditional way to enjoy calvados is between meals as 'Trou Nourmand' to help digestion and appetite. Serve 1 or 2 centilitres in a small glass. Calvados can be served as aperitif, blended in drinks, between meals, as digestive or with coffee.

Well-made calvados should naturally be reminiscent of apples and pears, balanced with flavours of ageing. You will notice that the less aged calvados distinguishes itself with its fresh apple and pear aromas. The longer the calvados is under the influence of oak, the more the taste resembles that of any other aged brandy. This balance is a matter of taste; some like the fruity style, others prefer when the smoother flavours of ageing is given space.

Buying and tasting calvados, you will find that most calvados is blends of different ages. The choice in quality and style lies in the producer and the age of the blend. Producers usually offer a range of blends and occasionally vintages.

Calvados is a perfect match for a fine cigar.

Calvados

Mouth · Flavour · Bouquet
Palate · Aroma

Body: Alcohol, Rich/full, Light, Mellow, Length, Tannins

Floral: Apple blossom, Rose, Jasmine, Violet

Taste: Acidic, Sweet, Salty, Bitter

Fruit
- Fresh / Citrus: Pear, Peach, Apricot, Plum, Prune, Lemon, Orange, Lime, Grape
- Dried: Apricot, Peach, Raisins, Plum, Muscat, Apple
- Apple: Sweet, Baked, Red, Green, Crisp, Sour
- Citrus

Other: Mushroom, Chemical, Tar, Vinegary, Charcoal

Spice/herb: Clove, Aniseed, Nutmeg, Cinnamon, Coffee, Fennel, Pepper, Tea

Wood: Oak, Cedar, Sap, Resin, Sandalwood, Leather, Tobacco, Burnt toast, Toasted nut, Bread, Brioche

Toast: Apple-pie, Honey, Wood, Sweet, Toast

Sweet: Caramel, Port, Sherry, Butterscotch, Apple butter, Vanilla bean, Molasses, Butter, Chocolate, Liquorice

Nut: Hazelnut, Flor, Chestnut, Almond, Cashew, Walnut

35

Calvados

'Fine', 'Trois étoiles', ***,
'Trois pommes' and
'Originel'

• Eye	Neutral with a pale yellow shade.
• Nose and palate	Straight fruity apple and pear combined with some roundness, vanilla and toast from ageing.
• How to enjoy	In cooking, blended in drinks, well chilled as 'vodka shot' or with ice as an aperitif.

Aged calvados

'Vieux', 'Réserve',
and young calvados
Domfrontais

• Eye	Straw yellow with light amber.
• Nose and palate	Fresh apples and pears, dried apricot, vanilla and toffee.
• How to enjoy	As fruity all-round calvados with tones of ageing. Serve as a aperitif, digestive, plain, on ice or with coffee. Good base for drinks and chilled for vodka 'shot'.

Longer aged calvados

'V.O.', 'Vieille Réserve' and 'V.S.O.P.'

Very old calvados

'Extra', 'X.O.', 'Napoléon', 'Hors d'Age', 'Age Inconnu' and older vintages

• Eye	Yellow with darker strokes of amber and gold.
• Nose and palate	Intense with concentration of tangy apples and dried apricots balanced with butterscotch, nutty and chocolate aromas.
• How to enjoy	As digestive, with cigar, dark chocolate or desserts.

• Eye	Gold, darker brown with orange elements and red mahogany.
• Nose and palate	Delicate with concentration of aged apples and dried apricots balanced with butterscotch, nut and chocolate aromas.
• How to enjoy	Rare and exciting calvados for special moments.

Gastronomy

Only idiots are not gourmands/Norman wisdom

Thanks to all the apples, pears, cider, calvados and pommeau available - many of the Norman chefs like to flavour with them. Young calvados with 'fresh' tones of apple works very well in most recipes. Longer aged calvados with its woody tone is not preferred in most cases.

Easy creamy calvados sauce

This sauce tastes delicious with white meat like chicken, veal or fish.
4-6 servings
1.5 dl (5 oz) double cream
4 dl (10 oz) stock (veal or chicken for meat, fish for fish)
8 finely chopped mushrooms
3 cl (1 oz) of calvados
1 teaspoon of cornflour
Simmer the cream, stock and mushrooms for 20 minutes. Whisk the cornflour with the calvados and stir in the sauce. Season with salt and pepper.

Calvados and pepper sauce

Excellent with grilled meat, duck, venison or other game.
4-6 servings
1 tbsp tomato puree
1.5 dl (5 oz) double cream
4 dl (10 oz) brown stock
3 cl (1 oz) of calvados
1 tsp of cornflour
Salt and freshly ground black pepper
In a saucepan fry the

Farm made cider vinegar and cider jelly can be found all over Normandy at cellar door sales and shops.

tomato puree in some butter for a minute. Add the cream and stock and simmer for 20 minutes. Whisk the cornflour with the calvados and stir into the sauce. Season with salt and freshly ground black pepper and serve.

Calvados Teriyaki sauce

Use as a glace or serve as sauce with any grilled or fried food.

4-6 servings
4 tbsp honey
1 dl (3 oz) of Japanese soy sauce (like Kikkoman)
6 cl (2 oz) of calvados
1 teaspoon of corn flour

Whisk all the ingredients together in a saucepan, stir and simmer for a couple of minutes. Season with salt and freshly ground white pepper.

Fruit in calvados

A perfect gift or easy dessert served with crème caramel; vanilla ice cream, meringues and whipped cream; panna

Sauces from the left: easy creamy calvados sauce, calvados and pepper sauce and calvados Teriyaki sauce. Grilled filet of beef with potato gratin and calvados and pepper sauce. Grilled chicken on apples and easy creamy calvados sauce with bacon.

cotta or lemontarte.
1 glass container with lid
1 part sugar
4 parts of rinsed cherries or rinsed plums
1 bottle of calvados

Mix cherries or plums with sugar in the container. Cover with calvados and leave to mature for a couple of days. Keeps for a very long time.

Calvados in drinks

Surprise with exciting drinks

Cocktails have a long tradition in Normandy. Yet calvados is quite rare in drinks.

• Most of the drinks that contain brandy will work very well with calvados.

• Young and less aged calvados can replace non-aged spirits like vodka, tequila or rum.

• Well aged calvados can replace aged spirits like rum or cognac. They are also suited to being served on their own with cigar, 'on the rocks' or plain with soda.

• Pommeau is a nice aperitif or companion to desserts. Served with ice it turns into a long drink and with sparkling wine or cider an aperitif.

• Liqueurs of apple have a sweet apple aroma and a nice change from other liqueurs used in cocktails.

• 'Calvados cream' can be served plain over ice or used in drinks like any other cream liqueur.

Sparkling cocktail with calvados
1/10 calvados
9/10 sparkling wine or cider
Use a flute or saucer. Add calvados and top with sparkling wine or cider.

Vanilla apple sip
30 ml (1 oz) vodka vanilla
30 ml (1 oz) calvados
30 ml (1 oz) liqueur of apples
Shake with ice and serve in a martini glass with a slice of apple.

Calvarita

45 ml (1 1/2 oz) calvados
15 ml (1/2 oz) Cointreau
30 ml (1 oz) lime juice

Rub the rim of a cocktail glass with lime juice, turn the glass upside down and sprinkle with salt. Shake all the ingredients with ice, strain into the salt-rimmed glass.

Cosmo calva

30 ml (1 oz) calvados
15 ml (1/2 oz) Cointreau
15 ml (1/2 oz) cranberry juice
A splash of lime juice

Shake ingredients with ice and serve in a martini glass with a wedge of lime.

Calva sweet and sour

30 ml (1 oz) calvados
30 ml (1 oz) liqueur of apples
30 ml (1 oz) lime juice

Add calvados, liqueur and lime juice to a shaker half-filled with ice. Shake and strain into a highball glass filled to ¾ with ice cubes. Top with Sprite or 7-Up.

Adams appledos

30 ml (1 oz) calvados
30 ml (1 oz) Galliano
Cider

Place ice in a highball glass, add the calvados and Galliano and fill up with cider.

Hot apple punch - mulled cider

1 part calvados
3 parts dry cider

Warm the cider with a stick of cinnamon, 2 whole cloves and serve with brown sugar to taste.

The cellars

Seek out some of the major producers

There are many small producers left out in this directory. Some are marked on the map at the end of this book. Find out more in the larger *Calvados – the world's premier apple brandy* (also by Henrik Mattsson).

BOULARD S.A.C.B.
14130 COQUAINVILLIERS
Tel: 02 31 48 24 00
www.calvados-boulard.com

Award winning high quality calvados Pays d'Auge made with attention to tradition on large scale. The homepage, estate and cellars of Boulard are well worth a visit. Everything about Boulard is well organized and enjoyable if you don't mind the tourist approach. Boulard is one of the largest exporters of

calvados Pays d'Auge and 80 percent of their produce ends up on tables all over the world. Their homepage is informative and you can read that the Boulard family have run the company for 170 years, take a look at old labels or indulge in recipes and much more. Boulard's cellar door sales contain a unique restaurant called 'Bistrot Normand' with tables inside giant barrels and Norman dressed staff serving traditional food (with lots of cream and cider). Guided tours. Their range includes, apart from cider and pommeau, Grand Solage (3-5 years), XO (8-15 years), Hors d'Age (10 – 20 years), Vintages (for example 1973) Carafe 21 years old. (D3)

BUSNEL and ANÉE
Route de Lisieux, 27260 CORMEILLES
Tel: 02 32 57 38 80
cormeilles.com/Partenaires/ busnel (not official sites but contain useful info)
 The distillery in Cormeilles was built in 1910. Today it also contains a visiting facility with cellar door sales, tours and tasting room. It is the home of the brands Busnel and Anée, both high quality calvados Pays d'Auge and pommeau with ranges including price winning Hors d'Age, aged for 15 years in small oak barrels. As early as 1820 Ernest

A cow and her calf in the orchard near the Camut mansion. The grandson of the late Adrien Camut with a bottle of calvados from his ancestors.

Busnel launched an apple brandy named 'calvados' in Pont-l'Evêque. George Anée founded Anée in 1919. Several generations of expertise and tradition have given Busnel and Anée individual personalities. Generally speaking, for Busnel, the cider is distilled longer, thus emphasis in the taste will be for fruit. Regarding Anée a prolonged maturation makes it possible to curtail distillation, focusing on the mellow taste from oak ageing. Range includes Fine (3 years), Vieille Réserve Pays d'Auge (4 years), Hors d'Age (10 years), Vieille Réserve Prestige Pays d'Auge (12 years), 1963, pommeau and cider. (D3)

CAMUT

Domaine de Sémainville
27210 LA LANDE SAINT LEGER
Tel: 02 32 57 82 01
Agathe.camut@wanadoo.fr

Welcome visitors by appointment. Is quite hard to find but worth it. Very high quality award-winning and old calvados available. Genuine Pays d'Auge mansion, orchards and cellars. Represented at several fine restaurants including the Taillevent in Paris. Around 15 000 bottles (50 percent export). The Camut family has made calvados for generations. 50 years ago Adrien Camut was one of the pioneers to sell 'calvados degustation', good tasting calvados to restaurants (instead of the usual, low quality and cheap Café-Calva). The Camut family have about 4000 traditional high-stem apple trees just inside the Pays d'Auge. The blends

are as natural as possible and are bottled unfiltered. 2001 was the first year that Camut released their pommeau - Aperitif Normand. The range also includes the 6, 12, 18 year olds; Reserve de Semainville (a blend of 25-30 year old), Reserve d'Adrien (35-40 years), Prestige (40-50 years) and Rareté (old enough). (D3)

CHATEAU DU BREUIL

14130 LE-BREUIL-EN-AUGE
Tel: 02 31 65 60 00
www.chateau-breuil.fr

Cellar door sales. Guided tours and well made home page. Open for seminars, functions, receptions and incentives. Award winning calvados Pays d'Auge, cider and pommeau of very high quality. Chateau du Breuil is one of the regions most beautiful 'chateau'. The

cellar door sales and tasting facilities are situated next to the chateau with a view over a manmade lake. Chateau du Breuil manages very well in making traditional-made calvados Pays d'Auge on large scale. Range includes from fruity Fine (2 years)

One of the elegant bottles and the historic surroundings from Chateau du Breuil.

and VSOP (4 years) to more balanced, woody and exquisite calvados of 8, 12, 15 and 20 – 25 years (Réserve des Seigneurs XO). Du Breuil also bottles even more prestigious calvados like calvados Royal (a calvados with no age made from calvados with exceptional potential that the cellar master has put aside during his tastings); calvados N°14 (named after the number of the French department: this calvados is a tribute and assembled from small oak barrels); calvados Fût N°146 (a cask strength 12 year old calvados Pays d'Auge taken exclusively from barrel N°146). Réserve de la Châtelaine (a 'feminine' blend of round and flowery calvados Pays d'Auge, Hors d'Age, especially marketed for ladies), pommeau and calvados liqueur 'Coeur du Breuil' also available. (D3)

CHRISTIAN DROUIN - 'COEUR DE LION'

Le Lieu Saint-Pierre, 14130 COUDRAY RABUT
Tel: 02 31 64 30 05
www.coeur-de-lion.com

Agricultural producer (and merchant) of high quality calvados Pays d'Auge, cider and pommeau. Extensive range of vintages. Cellar sales. Guided tours.
In 1960, Christian Drouin senior purchased the estate of Fiefs Sainte-Anne on the hill of Gonneville close to Honfleur. It was not until 1979 that stocks were considered sufficient to start marketing and selling the

Photo Drouin

47

The cellars at Domaine Coeur de Lion. At the left corner of the building you can see one of the stills.

calvados. Today Drouin has built a reputation worldwide as one of the top producers and 70 percent of the production is exported to 40 countries, mostly to USA, Japan, Germany, Scandinavia and Italy.

In 1991-92 Christian Drouin

moved to Coudray-Rabut close to Pont-l'Evêque. Originally an old stud farm from the 17th century he baptized it Domaine Coeur de Lion and carefully restored it. Today it contains production and ageing facilities (there are barrels everywhere), a house for visiting parties, a tasting room and sales room.

Drouin produces not only high quality traditional blends but also an extensive range of vintages from family stocks and a collection of very old calvados acquired when estates of well-known producers have been sold. The range includes 'Pomme Prisonnière', Fine (3 years), Réserve des Fiefs (4 years), V.S.O.P., Hors d'âge (+15 years) and 25 Ans d'Age (+25 years). The vintages include 1939 to 1984 and each shows a unique personality. Some examples are the 1976, -77 and -79 partly aged in Sherry barrels; the classic balanced 1973; the 1970 aged partly in Port and Sherry barrels and the 1969 with hints from Port barrels. (D3)

CLOS D'ORVAL

14310 AMAYE S/SEULLES
Tel: 02 31 77 02 87

Agricultural producer along the 'route de traditions'. Award-winning

high quality cider, calvados and pommeau. Cellar door sales, guided tours and a small museum. 20 ha of orchards with tradition back to the eighteenth century. Range includes Fine (2 years), Vieux (4 years), Vieille Réserve (8 years), Hors d'Age (+10 years) and 15, 20 and 35 years old calvados. (B3)

COMTE DE LAURISTON

Chais du Verger Normand
Rue du Mont-St-Michel, 61700
DOMFRONT
Tel: 02 33 38 53 96

Cellar door sales. Comte de Lauriston is a range of several vintages of high quality award-winning calvados Domfrontais. The calvados is distilled by around 100 farmers in the area and bought by the cellar. The emphasis is on fruit, at least 30 percent pears are used, and second hand oak barrels are used to give a discrete tone of ageing. Chais du Verger Normand

was created in 1962 with help from Comte de Lauriston because of an agreement between the farmers and the authorities to solve a nightly controversy involving home brewing. Since 1992, the brand Comte de Lauriston has been marketed, co-produced and represented by Christian Drouin at Coeur de Lion. The range includes vintages from 1961, 1963, 1964, 1968 to 1975, 1977, 1978, 1980, 1982 and 1983, 20 years old, VSOP (5 years), Hors d'Age (10 years), 'captive apple –pear', pommeau and cider. (C5)

At vertical tasting of different vintages at Comte de Lauriston, you'll find that each has its unique qualities. Domaine du Coquerel (right) is situated in the Domfront area and only use apples despite the fact that the surrounding area is classic pear country.

COQUEREL, Domaine du Manoir du Coquerel, 50000 MILLY
Tel: 02 33 79 02 20
www.calvados-coquerel.com

Cellar door sales and guided tours. Award winning and high quality calvados with an extensive range and some very old calvados. The Manor house of Coquerel is located in Milly, near Saint Hilaire du Harcouët and

Domfront. Traditionally an area where calvados is made with pears, Coquerel's focus is on apples. The history of Coquerel begins in 1937 and the founder René Gilbert made it into one of the first houses of calvados. The French President has rewarded the estate for its quality five times. In the cellars, over 2000 small barrels (300 to 600 litres) of Limousin oak are aged. An annual distillation of 2500 hl pure alcohol is slowly transformed to an extensive range of calvados. 55 percent of it

is exported to European countries, mostly Germany, but also to Asia and the United States. Range includes the brands Coquerel (Fine to XO) and Marquis de la Pomme (15 years and vintage 1967), Pomme d'Eve (trapped apple) and some other present bottles. Duc d'Arthour and Baron de la Touque are two other brands associated with Coquerel. Pommeau, Crème de calvados and Liqueur de Pomme are also available. (B5)

DARON

Office: 191 Ave du General Leclerc, 78220 VIROFLAY, FRANCE
Tel: 01 30 83 22 44, Fax: 01 30 24 52 72
www.gafrance.com/daron
No visits. Brand by Gabriel & Andreu who is a French corporation specializing in the production and marketing of fine spirits with a focus on cognac with sales in over 45 countries. Daron is a brand of calvados Pays d'Auge sold as Fine (5 years) or XO (18 years).

DAVID

Manoir de Sens, 14430 BEUVRON-EN-AUGE
Tel: 02 31 79 23 05, www. manoirdesens.com
    Bed and breakfast. Cellar door sales of calvados Pays d'Auge, pommeau and cider "Cru de

Cambremer" along 'the road of cider'. Beuvron is a charming Pays d'Auge village and home to Maison David. Very old calvados available. (D3)

DAUFRESNE, Philippe

14100 OUILLY LE VICOMTE
Tel: 02 31 62 29 84
    Agricultural producer. Cellar door sales. Award winning high quality calvados and calvados Pays d'Auge, cider and pommeau. Distillery in a

typical Norman building and a cellar from 18th century. Cider also sold at 'Aux trois Damoiselles' in Beuvron-en-Auge (www. auxtroisdamoiselles. com). (D3)

DESFRIECHES Serge
Le Lieu Chéri, 14100 OUILLY LE VICOMTE
Tel: 02 31 61 11 71
   Farm made 'fermier' calvados Pays d'Auge, pommeau and cider of high quality. Cellar door sales in traditional farm. Bed and breakfast and 'gites', holiday cottages.

DES DEUX-SAPINS, EARL
JAOUEN, Florence and Philippe
Ferme de Ponctey, 27500 TRIQUEVILLE
Tel: 02 32 42 10 37
E-mail: ponctey@rurintel.fr.eu.org
   High quality farm made 'fermier' calvados, pommeau and cider. Award

winning VSOP. Bed and breakfast. Cellar door sales. (D2)

DES GRIMAUX, EARL
PACORY, Frédéric and Catherine
61350 MANTILLY
Tel: 02 33 30 81 40
   Farm made calvados Domfrontais of high quality. Cellar door sales. Frederic Pacory took over the family farm, the Domaine des Grimaux, at the beginning of the 1990s. His father produced calvados, as did his grandfather. Range includes price winning Hors d'Age +10 years and a VSOP around 4-5 years. (B5)

DESVOYE, Gérard
Le Lieu Gris
Saint Aubin Libizay, 143 40 CAMBREMER
Tel: 02 31 65 11 94
   Cellar door sales. Farm made calvados, pommeau and cider of high quality in centre of Pays D'Auge. Guided visits of cellar, press and distillery. (D3)

DOMAINE DE LA MERITE

Jean MAIZERET, 27410 GOUTTIÈRES
Tel: 02 32 44 43 83, Fax: 02 32 44 23 89
http://merite.esds.com
Farm made 'fermier' (all made on farm) award-winning high quality calvados Hors d'Age (less than 3000 bottles a year) and VSOP from 'Pays de la Risle'. Can be ordered from homepage. (E3)

DUPONT, Domaine Louis

14430 VICTOT-PONTFOL
Tel: 02 31 63 24 24
www.calvados-dupont.com

Cellar door sales. Visit the distillery and cellars. Award winning agricultural made calvados, pommeau and cider of high quality. Etienne Dupont has been in charge of the Domain since 1980, when he took over from his father Louis and his grandfather Jules. Etienne learned the art of double distillation in

Two generations of Dupont - at the left Etienne beside Louis. The domain in Victot-Pontfol with shop, cellars and distillery (below) is open for visits.

Cognac. 1931 and some of the most recent vintages and blends are represented at many restaurants, among them the Taillevent in Paris. The Dupont range is not only high quality, but has a classic and elegant, yet modern 'look' as well. The range includes Original 'Générique' (2

years), Vieille Réserve, VSOP (8 years), Hors d'Age (10–12 years), 1972, 1974 (non-reduced), 1976, 1962, Captive Apple, pommeau, cider and vinegar. (D3)

FERMICALVA

Le Grand Chemin, 50540 ISIGNY-LE-BUAT

Tel: 02 33 48 00 16

Cellar door sales. Traditional and agricultural made quality calvados from 3 to 40 years old, calvados Domfrontais, cider and pommeau. The range includes brands like Fermicalva, Pere Thomas and Pere Mathieu. (B4)

FERME DE L'HERMITIERE
COULOMBIER, Jean-Luc, 50320 ST-JEAN-DES-CHAMPS

Norman dog kennel and bottles outside the cellar door sales at Fermicalva in the Domfront area.

Tel: 02 33 61 31 51
www.ferme-hermitiere.com

Educational farm. Cellar door sales. Agricultural made calvados, pommeau and cider. Cider farm passed father to son for five generations. Museum of cider and farming. Range from 3 to 25 years old calvados. (A4)

GIARD, S.C.E.A.
14340 GRANDOUET
Tel/Fax: 02 31 63 02 40

Award winning high quality calvados Pays d'Auge for several generations. Cellar door sales after agreement. Range includes 'Trois etoiles'

(4 years), 'Hors d'Age' (around 13 years), 'Plus de 15 ans' (around 17 years), 'Plus de 20 ans' (around 22 years) and vintage 1967. (D3)

GONTIER, Victor, S.C.E.A.
Langle, 50720 SAINT GEORGES DE ROUELLEY
Tel: 02 33 65 34 03

Cellar door sales. Agricultural calvados Domfrontais of high quality. Production

'fermier' – all done on farm. Range includes vintages like 1992, Vieille Reserve, 1970 and Grande Reserve, 1965. (B5)

GROULT, Roger
Route des calvados, 14290 ST-CYR-DU-RONCERAY
Tel: 02 31 63 71 53
www.groult.esc-brest.fr

Agricultural made calvados Pays D'Auge of very high quality. Cellar door sales at traditional mansion 'Clos de la Hurvanière' in the heart of the Pays d'Auge. Four generations of the Groult family have made calvados. In 1850, Pierre Groult started selling calvados. The property consists of 15 hectares of traditional high-stem apple trees and 8 hectares of 'half' high-stem apple trees. Additional fruit are also

The cellar (left) dedicated to the grandfather of Jean Pierre Groult. There are also cellars dedicated to his father and great-grandfather.

bought from neighbours. Groult philosophy is to use small stills for concentration and wood fire for a gentle non-aggressive heat. The range includes the 'Ancestral

Reserve' from the cellar of Pierre Groult (great-grandfather); 'Doyen d'Age' (grandfather); 'Venerable' and 'Golden Age' from the cellars of Roger Groult; complemented with calvados Pays d'Age of 15, 8 and 3 years of age. (D4)

HOULEY, Distillerie du
14590 OUILLY-DU-HOULEY
Tel: 02 31 63 63 46
E-mail: ribaude@club-internet.fr
 Cellar door sales with gift shop. Agricultural made calvados (Pays d'Auge) since several generations. Range includes very old calvados and brands of La Ribaude (Three stars, Vieux, Vieille Reserve, Hors d'Age and Prestige), De Querville and La Paquine. (D3)

HUARD, Michel
Le Pertyer, 61100
CALIGNY
Tel: 02 33 96 41 87

Agricultural
producer north of
Domfront since five
generations. Huard
is represented at the
famous restaurant
Taillevent in Paris
and Tokyo, where
they also have a 1893
vintage. The Huard
calvados symbolizes
traditionally made
'fermier' calvados
from 'haut-tiges',
high-stem orchards
with several (in
this case around
30) varieties of apples and a small
production of 3 - 4000 bottles.
Range includes for example "Le
Pertyer", XO, vintage 1982 - 86 and
Hors d'Age. (C5)

HUBERT
Les Vergers de la
Morinière
61230 LA
FRESNAIE FAYEL
Tel: 02 33 35 51 13
E-mail:
hubertmchl@aol.
com

Bed and breakfast.
Cellar door sales.
Agricultural made
high quality calvados
Pays d'Auge, pommeau, cider and
liqueur 'Poire au calvados'. Range
includes old vintages including
1965, 1987–99 and award-
winning
Hors d'Age
and VSOP.
(D5)

HUET ✓
Manoir La Brière des Fontaines,
14340 CAMBREMER
Tel: 02 31 63 01 09
www.calvados-huet.com

Cellar door sales in the Cambremer

'capital of cider'. Guided tours. Agricultural made calvados Pays d'Auge with a range of 3 – 30 years of very high quality. Cider, pommeau, vinegar, jelly and much more in the shop. At the 'La Brière des Fontaines' manor, the Huet family have made cider and calvados for five generations and won many medals. Huet is represented with many famous restaurateurs like Bocuse, Taillevent and Rostang. Belongs to the 'Cru de Cambremer' which is a government certification guaranteeing quality. (D3)

The Huet mansion in Cambremer. Next to it is the distillery and cellar door sales open for visits.

Tel: 02 31 63 50 33
www.cclf.fr
Founded in 1919 the CCLF makes pommeau and high quality calvados brands: Ecusson, La Traque, Henri d'Osne and Henry-Gérard, ranging from 2–42 years old. The Ecusson brand is a range of fruity calvados. The Pays d'Auge range is made of award-winning VSOP and Hors d'Age produced according to traditional methods. Henri d'Osne

LA FERMIERE
CCLF or CIDRERIE DU CALVADOS S.A.
Route de Lisieux, 14140 LIVAROT

brand has an elegant labelling with a range up to and over 20 years old. The Henry-Gérard brand is high quality VSOP, XO or Extra Very Old calvados in bottles or 'Jewel' decanters.

LEBREC, Bernard
14710 ENGLESQUEVILLE LA PERCEE
Tel: 02 31 22 70 72
E-mail: bernard.lebrec@free.fr
Farm made calvados. Cellar door sales of a limited 1000 bottles. The farms location is in an old stone mansion not far from the coast. (B2)

LECOMPTE
NOTRE-DAME-DE-COURSON, 14140
Tel: 02 31 48 24 07
www.calvados-lecompte.com
Award winning calvados Pays d'Auge of high quality. The distillery 'la Morinière' and cellars in Notre-Dame-de-Courson will be open for visits. You can also buy and taste the Lecompte range at wine specialists and shops in Caen, Rouen, le Havre and Deauville. In 1923 Alexandre Lecompte, an apple merchant in Gournay-en-Bray, started to sell the brand 'Lecompte, Rosée de Lisieux'. In 1955, the first aged Lecompte aged at 'Ferme de la Bascule' was launched with success among 'connoisseurs'. In 1979 the farm at Notre-Dame-de-Courson was bought with a substantial

The distillery of Lecompte is a discreet farm at Notre-Dame-de-Courson. It hides a substantial amount of old stocks and two traditional stills for double distillation. The Originel (right) is a young but fruity and soft calvados from Lecompte – perfect for drinks. The cellar master Richard Prevel and Hervé Pellerin tasting at the cellars (Photo from Lecompte).

amount of old stocks. In 1981, Lecompte started to export and build an image as the fruity calvados. Their recent blend 'originel' is the most representative of this effort. 75 percent of production is exported. Lecompte use a blend of small and large oak casks, both new and old, some are sherry cask used for +12 years. Range includes the fruity 'Originel' (3 years), 5 years, Hors d'Age (8–10 years), 12, 15 and 20 years old. 'La Reinelle' is a calvados liqueur.

LELOUVIER, Christian
55 Rue Teinture, 61600 LA
FERTE MACE
Tel: 02 33 37 00 95, Fax: 02
33 30 44 68
High quality agricultural
made calvados. Range
includes vintages like 1960,
-62 and -70; Hors d'Age
(25 years old), the brands
Guillaume de Normandie
and calvados Pays d'Auge
Chevallier Arthur. (C5)

LEMORTON, Roger
Le Pont Barabé, 61350
MANTILLY
Tel: 02 33 38 76 60

Traditional farm. Cellar door
sales. High quality agricultural made
calvados Domfrontais, pommeau
and cider. Award winning calvados
Domfrontais Hors d'Age. Roger
Lemorton is the fifth generation and
together with his son, Didier, now
runs the domain. The property is
planted with both apple and pear
trees. The appellation constitutes

at least 30 percent of
pears but at Lemorton
a larger amount is used.
The range includes
among others 'Réserve',
10-Year-Old, 1976,
1970, 1973, 1963,
1955, 1942, 1926 and
Rarete Lemorton
'Domfrontais (about
100 years old). (B5)

LE PERE JULES
Route de Dives, 14100 ST-
DESIR
Tel: 02 31 61 14 57

Brand by agricultural
producer since 1919 (three
generations of the Desfrièches
family). Traditionally made calvados
Pays d'Auge of high quality. Cellar
door sales just outside Lisieux with
cellar, press and distillery open
for visit. Around 40 hectares of
traditional high-stem orchards with
40 varieties of apples. Stills heated
with wood and calvados aged in
mostly old oak barrels. Range

Normal and magnum bottles from Le Père Jules north of Lisieux.

includes 3, 5, 10 and 20 years old. Cider, pommeau and some very old calvados also available. On the opposite side of the road is the only 'tonnelerie' (cooperer), in Calvados, which is run by the Desfrièches as well. (D3)

LEROYER, Gérard
Domaine de la Duretière, 53110 MELLERAY-LA-VALLÉE
Tel/Fax: 02 43 04 71 48
gleroyer@terre-net.fr
   Agricultural producer of high quality calvados Domfrontais. Musée du Cidre. Cellar door sales. President

Producteurs calvados Domfrontais. (C6)

LES REMPARTS
LECORNU,
Francois
4, rue Bourbesneur,
14400 BAYEUX
Tel: 02 31 92 50 40
www.bayeux-bandb.
com
   Cellar door sales in an eighteenth century mansion in central Bayeux next to world square Charles De Gaulle. Visit the underground cellar. Bed and breakfast. Farm made calvados, pommeau and cider of high quality for three generations. Range includes 'Fine' (2 years), 'Vieille Reserve' (4 years) and 'Hors D'Age', a blend of 6 to 12 years. Small production of 1000–1500 bottles. (B3)

LES VERGERS DE CHAMP-HUBERT
JOUI, Bénédicte and Raymond
Route de Beaulieu, 61190 IRAI

Tél: 2 33 34 21 58

www.champ-hubert.com

Cellar door sales. Bed and breakfast. Farm made calvados, cider and pommeau. Visit the Champ-Hubert orchards that are spread on 30 ha which represents 16.000 apple-trees with 20 different varieties. (E5)

MACREL, Joël

Manoir d'Angoville, 14430 CRICQUEVILLE-EN-AUGE

Tel: 02 31 79 26 57

Cellar door sales. Farm made calvados, pommeau and cider south of Cabourg. Range includes 4 years and Hors d'Age of 8 years. (D3)

MANOIR DE QUERVILLE

COURTEMANCHE, 14140 PRÊTREVILLE

Tel: 02 31 32 31 88

Cellar door sales. Farm made calvados. Beautiful 'chateau' from

fifteenth century. Annually around 1000 bottles of calvados Pays d'Auge (17 years) of high quality. (D4)

MANOIR DU GRANDOUET, GAEC.

GRANDVAL, François

14340 GRANDOUET

Tel: 02 31 63 08 73

Agricultural producer. Cellar door sales. Tasting and guiding in a very beautiful and old farm from sixteenth century with cellar and press.

Producer of award-winning cider 'Cru de Cambremer', pommeau and calvados Pays d'Auge along 'the road of cider' near Cambremer. (D3)

MANOIR D'APREVAL

14600 PENNEDEPIE

Tel: 02 31 14 88 24

www.apreval.com

Agricultural made calvados of high quality, cider and pommeau. Cellar

Tasting with Louis Demanche and Agathe Letellier at the family-run Manoir D'Apreval.

door sales near Honfleur. Manoir d'Apreval is a beautiful, traditional mansion surrounded by high-stem orchards with around 17 varieties of apples. Cellar, distillery and press are open for visits. (D2)

MARTAYROL

Hameau d'Englesqueville
Le Lieu Mancel, 14340
CAMBREMER
Tel: 01 48 20 63 08
www.martayrol.com
    Centrally located cellars in

Cambremer in the heart of calvados. Brands include Vieux Porche, Commandeur Normand, Chauffe-Coeur and Pere Prudent. (D3)

MORIN

10, rue d'Ezy, 27540 IVRY-LA-BATAILLE
Tel: 02 32 36 40 01, Fax: 02 32 36 69 63
calvadosmorin@tiscali.fr
High quality calvados and calvados Pays d'Auge made with traditional fabrication methods.

Morin was founded in Vallé de Risle in 1889 and is run by the Viry family who succeeded the founder Pierre Morin. Situated in Ivry-la-Bataille, Morin have a distillery in 'Abbey de Theleme', an old building dating back to the fifteenth century. The calvados is stored in the extensive underground natural cellars dug into the chalky hills of the Eure valley – unique in the world of calvados. The humidity of these cellars allows a slow maturation resulting in a smooth calvados. The range includes 3, 6, 10, 15, 25 years old, vintages such as 1973 and rare bottles like the 'Age d'Or' and the 'Prestige' – sold in a bottle affected with noble rot! (F4)

PARC DU MOULIN, DENOLY

Ammeville, 14170 SAINT-PIERRE-SUR-DIVES
Tel: 02 31 20 62 67
rene-philippe.denoly@wanadoo.fr

Award winning calvados, pommeau and cider 'fermier' – all done on the farm. Cellar door sales. Traditional farm with production from generations dating back to 1881. Biological produce. Range includes calvados Hors d'Age (20 years), Vieille

Réserve (6 years) and Extra Vieux (40 years). (D4)

PÈRE MAGLOIRE

Route de Trouville, 14130 PONT-L'EVEQUE
Tel: 02 31 64 12 87
www.pere-magloire.com;
magloire@pere-magloire.com
Père Magloire was one of the first recognized calvados brands and its history can be traced back to 1821. Today it's one of the largest producers. Award winning high quality calvados. Visitor centre with cellar door sales, restaurant with tables inside barrels and museum of old trades. Range includes cider and calvados Fine, VSOP

Benoit Pellerin welcomes you to Père Magloire visitor centre and cellars. Back in the old days stone constructions, like the one found outside the Père Magloire visitor centre, were horse powered to crush the fruit before pressing.

(4 years), XO (10 years) and a 20 years old calvados; calvados Pays d'Auge Réserve de Gouberville (6 years) and calvados Domfrontais (3 years); Pom'ka (calvados cream), Pom'o (pommeau) and Pom's (an apple liqueur in the same style as the Basque 'liqueur de Manzana Verde'). Père Magloire also delivers a small part of the production to other companies who sell it with their label.

PIEDNOIR, Philippe
Ferme Belleau, 14140 NOTRE DAME DE COURSON
Tel: 02 31 32 30 15
Cellar door sales. Farm made cider Pays d'Auge (cidre fermier), calvados Hors d'Age and pommeau of high quality. Family run since 1856 in the south of Pays d'Auge.
(D4)

POMYPOM

Le nouveau monde, 14340
CAMBREMER
Tel: 02 31 32 94 05
www.pomypom.com

Agricultural made calvados, cider
and aperitifs of good quality since
the nineteenth century. The New
world domain (Le nouveau monde)
has 23 hectares of apple trees
chosen for their organic quality.
All of the production is made on
site. Range includes 3 Pommes (3
years), Vieux (5 years), Hors d'Age
(12 years), Cuvée of the domain (20
years), pommeau, sparkling cider and
aperitifs. (D3)

PREAUX

Domaine de la Vectière, 61350
MANTILLY
Tel: 02 33 38 70 48

Cellar door sales. Agricultural
made calvados with high quality
made of 80 percent apples and 20
percent pears. Range includes from
3–20 years old XO (calvados Pays
d'Auge from Ravigny). (B6)

SAPINIERE, Ferme de la
14710 SAINT-LAURENT-SUR-
MER
Tel: 02 31 22 40 51

Farm made
cider, calvados
and pommeau.
Cellar door sales,
mostly of cider
as only around
1500 bottles of
calvados (aged
3 years) are sold annually. Three
cellars to visit (cider, pommeau and
calvados). (B2)

TOUTAIN

La Couterie, 27210 BEUZEVILLE
Tel: 02 32 57 70 76

Agricultural made calvados, cider
and pommeau. Cellar door sales. Very
high quality award-winning and old
calvados Pays
d'Auge. Range
includes Fine
(3 years), Vieux
(8 years), Hors
d'Age (15 years),

Vielle Réserve (30 years) and Très vieille reserve (50 years old). Toutain use second-hand barrels to limit the impact of new oak, relying more on time for his calvados to mature. About 8–12 thousand bottles are sold each year, about 60 percent is exported. Toutain is represented at Michelin star restaurants such as Troisgros, Blanc, Loiseau, Savoy and others. (D2)

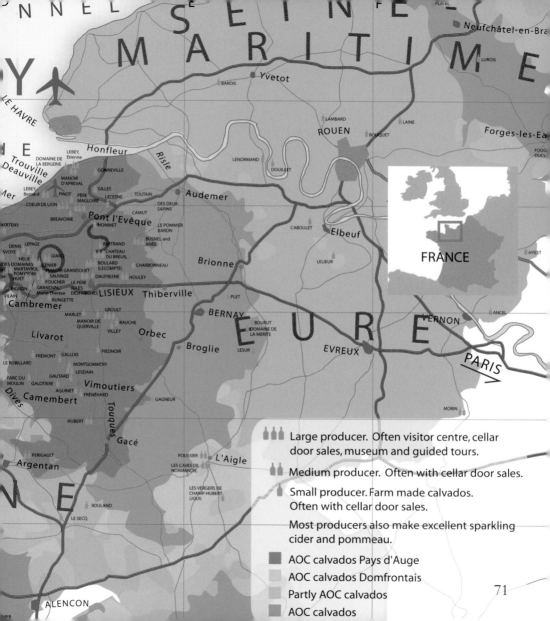